Ravioli Co That Exposes the Secrets

The Hidden Ravioli Recipes That No One Will Reveal to You

By: Angel Burns

© 2019 Angel Burns, All Rights Reserved.

License Notices

This book or parts thereof might not be reproduced in any format for personal or commercial use without the written permission of the author. Possession and distribution of this book by any means without said permission is prohibited by law.

All content is for entertainment purposes and the author accepts no responsibility for any damages, commercially or personally, caused by following the content.

Table of Contents

Homemade Ravioli Recipes 6

Recipe 1: Ravioli in Parmesan Sauce 7

Recipe 2: Ravioli Casserole 10

Recipe 3: Wild Mushrooms and Alfredo Ravioli 12

Recipe 4: Baked Cheesy Ravioli 14

Recipe 5: Roasted Red Pepper Ravioli 17

Recipe 6: Simple Ravioli Soup 21

Recipe 7: Ricotta Ravioli with Asparagus 24

Recipe 8: Deep Fried Ravioli 27

Recipe 9: Ravioli with Sausage 30

Recipe 10: Apple, Bacon and Spinach Ravioli 33

Recipe 11: Baked Pierogi Ravioli 36

Recipe 12: Ravioli and Roasted Zucchini 39

Recipe 13: Baked Broccoli Ravioli 42

Recipe 14: Pesto, Squash and Sage Ravioli 46

Recipe 15: Crabmeat Ravioli in Clam Sauce 49

Recipe 16: Three Bean Ravioli Minestrone 53

Recipe 17: Ravioli with Brown Butter and Roasted Squash 56

Recipe 18: Goat Cheese Stuffed Mint Ravioli 59

Recipe 19: Garlic and Herb Oil Ravioli 63

Recipe 20: Tuscan Ravioli with Tomato and Basil Sauce 65

Recipe 21: Ravioli and Vegetable Soup 67

Recipe 22: Cheese Ravioli with Cherry Tomato Sauce 70

Recipe 23: Cherry and Brown Butter Ravioli 74

Recipe 24: Pumpkin Ravioli with Gorgonzola Sauce ... 77

Recipe 25: Spinach Ravioli Lasagna 81

About the Author 84

Author's Afterthoughts 86

Homemade Ravioli Recipes

Recipe 1: Ravioli in Parmesan Sauce

This is a simple ravioli dish when you need something convenient to make for your family. Smothered in a creamy sauce, everybody will love it so much they will be begging for seconds.

Yield: 4 servings

Cooking Time: 15 minutes

Ingredient List:

- 1, 9 ounce of whole wheat cheese ravioli
- ¾ pound of shelled edamame
- 1 teaspoon of thyme, chopped
- ½ cup of reduced fat sour cream
- ½ cup of Parmesan cheese, shredded
- ½ teaspoons of black pepper

HHHHHHHHHHHHHHHHHHHHHHHHHHHHHHHHH

Instructions:

1. In a pot set over medium to high heat, fill with salted water. Allow to come to a boil. Add in the ravioli. Cook for 5 minutes or until soft.

2. Add in the shelled edamame. Cook for 1 to 2 minutes or until soft. Drain and set aside.

3. Reserve ¼ cup of the pasta liquid.

4. Add the ravioli into the pot. Add in the chopped thyme.

5. In a bowl, add in the sour cream, shredded Parmesan cheese and the reserved liquid. Season with a dash of salt and black pepper. Stir well to mix.

6. Pour the sauce over the ravioli. Toss gently to mix.

7. Serve immediately.

Recipe 2: Ravioli Casserole

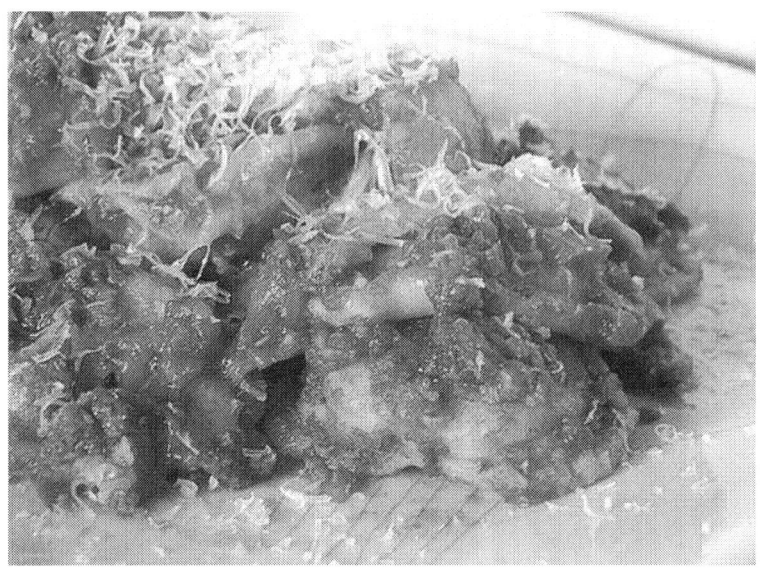

This is the perfect ravioli dish to make whenever you have a large group of people. One bite and they will be begging you for the recipe.

Yield: 6 to 8 servings

Cooking Time: 45 minutes

Ingredient List:

- 1, 26 ounce jar of spaghetti sauce, evenly divided
- 1, 25 ounce pack of cheese ravioli, cooked and evenly divided
- 2 cups of cottage cheese, evenly divided
- 4 cups of mozzarella cheese, shredded and divided
- ¼ cup of grated Parmesan cheese

HHHHHHHHHHHHHHHHHHHHHHHHHHHHHHH

Instructions:

1. In a baking dish, pour ½ cup of the spaghetti sauce.

2. Add in half of the cheese ravioli over the sauce. Pour 1 ¼ cups of the spaghetti sauce over the top.

3. Add 1 cup of cottage cheese and 2 cups of shredded mozzarella cheese over the top.

4. Repeat these layers once.

5. Sprinkle the grated Parmesan cheese.

6. Place into the oven to bake for 40 minutes at 350 degrees. Remove and set aside to cool for 10 minutes before serving.

Recipe 3: Wild Mushrooms and Alfredo Ravioli

This is a delicious ravioli dish that is appealing to both the eye and palette. Since it is made in a slow cooker, there is no other ravioli dish that is as easy to make as this one.

Yield: 8 servings

Cooking Time: 2 hours and 12 minutes

Ingredient List:

- 2, 15 ounce jars of alfredo sauce
- 2, 9 ounce packs of wild mushroom agnolotti pasta
- 1 cup of parmesan cheese, shredded
- 4 cups of grape tomatoes
- 1 cup of walnuts, toasted and cut into halves
- Dash of black pepper
- 4 cups of baby spinach
- Parmesan cheese, shredded and for garnish

HHHHHHHHHHHHHHHHHHHHHHHHHHHHHHHH

Instructions:

1. In a slow cooker, add in 1 cup of the alfredo sauce.

2. Add the pack of agnolotti pasta, ½ cup of shredded parmesan cheese, 2 cups of grape tomatoes and ½ cup of chopped walnuts. Repeat these layers once more.

3. Season with a dash of black pepper.

4. Top off with the remaining alfredo sauce.

5. Cover and cook on the highest setting for 2 hours.

6. Add in the baby spinach. Stir well to mix.

7. Serve.

Recipe 4: Baked Cheesy Ravioli

This is the perfect ravioli recipe you can make whenever you are in a hurry. It is so easy to make, you can have it ready on your kitchen table in just a matter of minutes.

Yield: 4 servings

Cooking Time: 15 minutes

Ingredient List:

- 1 ¼ cup of baby spinach
- 1 ½ cup of marinara sauce
- 1 ounce of sundried tomatoes
- ¾ cup of mozzarella cheese, shredded
- 2 Tablespoons of Parmesan cheese, grated
- 12 ounces of cheese ravioli

HHHHHHHHHHHHHHHHHHHHHHHHHHHHHHHH

Instructions:

1. Preheat the oven to 425 degrees.

2. In a colander set in the sink, add in the baby spinach.

3. In a bowl, add in the marinara sauce and tomatoes. Stir well to mix. In a separate bowl, add in the shredded mozzarella cheese and grated Parmesan cheese.

4. In a pot set over medium to high heat, fill with water. Allow to come to a boil. Add in the cheese ravioli. Cook for 2 to 3 minutes or until the ravioli begins to float to the surface. Drain the spinach in the same colander with the spinach. Set aside for 1 to 2 minutes or until the spinach wilts.

5. Transfer half of the spinach and cooked ravioli into the marinara mix. Toss well to coat.

6. Transfer into a baking dish. Sprinkle 1/3 of the cheese mix over the top. Add the remaining ravioli and remaining cheese.

7. Place into the oven to bake for 10 to 12 minutes.

8. Remove and serve immediately.

Recipe 5: Roasted Red Pepper Ravioli

This is a simple yet tasty ravioli dish whenever you are craving something on the spicy side. Serve with garlic bread for the tastiest results.

Yield: 4 servings

Cooking Time: 35 minutes

Ingredient List:

- 3 red bell peppers
- 2 to 3 Tablespoons of onion, chopped
- 2 Tablespoons of garlic, minced
- ¼ cup of basil
- 3 Tablespoons of extra virgin olive oil
- 1 ½ cup of half and half
- 1 teaspoon of cornstarch
- 1/3 cup of grated romano cheese
- 2 Tablespoons of butter
- Dash of salt and black pepper
- 1 pack of cheese ravioli, cooked

HHHHHHHHHHHHHHHHHHHHHHHHHHHHHHHHH

Instructions:

1. Preheat the oven to broil.

2. On a baking sheet, add the chopped red bell peppers. Drizzle the olive oil and toss well to coat. Place into the oven to broil for 5 minutes or until black. Transfer immediately into a paper bag and allow to steam for 5 to 10 minutes.

3. Remove the skin from the red bell peppers and cut into small pieces.

4. In a skillet set over medium heat, add in 1 tablespoon of olive oil. Add in the minced garlic, sliced basil, chopped red bell peppers and chopped onion. Stir well to mix. Cook for 10 minutes.

5. In a bowl, add in the cornstarch and half and half. Whisk until smooth in consistency.

6. Transfer the pepper mix into a blender. Blend on the highest setting until smooth in consistency. Pour back into the skillet. Add in the half and half mix. Stir well to incorporate.

7. Add in the grated romano cheese and butter. Season with a dash of salt and black pepper. Cook for 5 minutes.

8. Add in the ravioli and toss gently to mix.

9. Remove from heat and serve immediately.

Recipe 6: Simple Ravioli Soup

This is another delicious soup recipe you can make whenever you are feeling under the weather. It is great to make any night of the week.

Yield: 6 servings

Cooking Time: 35 minutes

Ingredient List:

- 2 Tablespoons of extra virgin olive oil
- 3 cloves of garlic, chopped
- 1 onion, chopped
- 4 cups of chicken broth
- 2 teaspoons of Italian seasoning
- 9 ounces of cheese ravioli
- 1, 28 ounce can of crushed tomatoes with juice
- 8 ounces of baby spinach, chopped

HHHHHHHHHHHHHHHHHHHHHHHHHHHHHHHH

Instructions:

1. In a pot set over medium heat, add in the olive oil. Add in the chopped garlic and chopped onion. Stir well to mix. Cook for 5 minutes or until translucent.

2. Add in the chicken broth and Italian seasoning. Allow to come to a boil.

3. Add in the cheese ravioli. Cook for 10 minutes or until the ravioli is cooked through.

4. Lower the heat to low. Add in the can of crushed tomatoes. Continue to cook for an additional 15 minutes.

5. Add in the chopped baby spinach. Cook for 1 minute or until wilted.

6. Season with a dash of salt and black pepper.

7. Remove from heat and serve immediately.

Recipe 7: Ricotta Ravioli with Asparagus

This is a simple and delicious ravioli dish that is perfect to make for any elegant occasion. Feel free to add in any vegetables you love to make this dish unique.

Yield: 6 servings

Cooking Time: 15 minutes

Ingredients for the ravioli:

- 1 cup of ricotta cheese
- ¼ cup of grated Pecorino Romano cheese
- 2 Tablespoons of flat leaf parsley, minced
- 1/8 teaspoons of salt
- 2 egg whites
- 48 round gyoza skins
- 6 quarts of water

Ingredients for the topping:

- 1 ½ Tablespoons of butter
- 2 cups of asparagus, thinly sliced
- ¼ teaspoons of salt
- 2 teaspoons of poppy seeds
- 1/3 cup of ricotta salata cheese, crumbled

HHHHHHHHHHHHHHHHHHHHHHHHHHHHHH

Instructions:

1. Prepare the ravioli. In a bowl, add in the ricotta cheese, grated pecorino romano cheese, chopped parsley, egg whites and dash of salt. Stir well until evenly blended.

2. On one gyoza skin, add 2 teaspoons of the ricotta mix into the center. Fold the skin of the gyoza over the filling. Crimp the edges to seal. Repeat with the remaining skins and filling.

3. Transfer onto a floured baking sheet.

4. In a pot set over medium to high heat, add in the 6 quarts of water. Allow to come to a boil. Add in the ravioli. Cook for 5 minutes. Drain and set the ravioli aside.

5. In a skillet set over medium heat, add in the butter. Add in the asparagus, ¼ cup of the ravioli liquid and dash of salt. Cook for 3 minutes or until crispy.

6. Add in the poppy seeds. Cook for an additional 30 seconds.

7. Add in the ravioli. Toss gently to mix.

8. Remove from heat. Sprinkle the ricotta salata cheese over the top and serve.

Recipe 8: Deep Fried Ravioli

This is a delicious festival dish I know even the pickiest of eaters will fall in love with. One bite and everyone who tries it will become hooked.

Yield: 4 servings

Cooking Time: 25 minutes

Ingredient List:

- 1 quart of vegetable oil
- 1 cup of all-purpose flour
- 2 eggs, beaten
- 1 cup of plain breadcrumbs
- ½ cup of grated parmesan cheese, evenly divided
- 2 Tablespoons of dried oregano
- 2 Tablespoons of dried basil
- 1 tablespoon of dried thyme
- 2 teaspoons of powdered garlic
- 1 teaspoon of salt
- ½ teaspoons of black pepper
- 12 cheese ravioli, for serving

HHHHHHHHHHHHHHHHHHHHHHHHHHHHHHHH

Instructions:

1. In a pot set over medium to high heat, add the vegetable oil. Heat the oil until it reaches 350 degrees.

2. In a shallow dish, add the all-purpose flour. In a separate shallow dish, add in the beaten eggs. In a third shallow dish, add in the plain breadcrumbs, ¼ cup of grated parmesan cheese, dried oregano, dried thyme, dried basil, powdered garlic, dash of salt and black pepper. Stir gently to mix.

3. Toss the ravioli in the flour. Dip into the beaten eggs and roll gently in the breadcrumb mix. Repeat with the remaining ravioli. Thread 3 of the coated ravioli onto skewers.

4. Add the ravioli skewers into the hot oil. Fry for 4 to 5 minutes or until golden. Transfer onto a plate lined with paper towels to drain.

5. Sprinkle the remaining ¼ cup of grated parmesan cheese over the ravioli.

6. Serve.

Recipe 9: Ravioli with Sausage

This a hearty and delicious ravioli that every meat lover in your home will love. It is a simple yet filling dish that can be made for dinner any night of the week.

Yield: 5 servings

Cooking Time: 15 minutes

Ingredient List:

- 2 red bell peppers, thinly sliced
- 1 onion, thinly sliced
- 1 pack of Italian chicken sausage, cooked
- 2 packs of cheese ravioli
- 2 teaspoons of vegetable oil
- 1 teaspoon of garlic, minced
- ½ cup of chicken broth
- 10 basil leaves

HHHHHHHHHHHHHHHHHHHHHHHHHHHHHHHHH

Instructions:

1. In a pot set over medium to high heat, add in 4 cups of water. Add in the cheese ravioli. Cook for 2 to 3 minutes or until the ravioli begins to float to the surface. Drain and set aside.

2. In a skillet set over medium to high heat, add in the sliced red bell peppers and sliced onions. Cook for 5 minutes or until soft.

3. Add in the sausage. Cook for 2 minutes. Add in the minced garlic. Cook for an additional 30 seconds.

4. Add in the chicken broth.

5. Remove the skillet from heat. Add in the cheese ravioli. Toss gently to mix.

6. Serve with a garnish of the basil over the top.

Recipe 10: Apple, Bacon and Spinach Ravioli

This surprising ravioli dish is made with a flavor I guarantee you have never had before. It is a satisfying meal your family will love.

Yield: 4 servings

Cooking Time: 20 minutes

Ingredient List:

- 16 ounces of cheese ravioli
- 6 slices of bacon
- 2 Tablespoons of extra virgin olive oil
- 2 cloves of garlic, minced
- 1 Braeburn apple, chopped
- 1 bunch of spinach
- Dash of salt and black pepper
- 1 tablespoon of lemon juice

HHHHHHHHHHHHHHHHHHHHHHHHHHHHHHHHH

Instructions:

1. Prepare the cheese ravioli according to the directions on the package.

2. In a skillet set over medium heat, add in the bacon. Cook for 6 to 8 minutes or until crispy. Transfer onto a plate lined with paper towels to drain. Once cooled, crumble the bacon.

3. Clean the skillet. Set back over medium heat. Add in 1 tablespoon of olive oil. Add in the minced garlic. Cook for 1 to 2 minutes or until golden. Add in the chopped Braeburn apple. Cook for an additional minute.

4. Add in the spinach. Season with a dash of salt and black pepper. Cook for 1 to 2 minutes or until wilted.

5. Add in the lemon juice, crumbled bacon and ravioli. Toss gently to mix.

6. Serve immediately.

Recipe 11: Baked Pierogi Ravioli

This is the Italian version of a Polish dish that is impossible to resist. Covered in a creamy sauce, you will quickly become hooked on it.

Yield: 4 servings

Cooking Time: 40 minutes

Ingredient List:

- 1, 16 ounce pack of potato and onion pierogies
- 2 bacon slices, chopped
- 2 cloves of garlic, minced
- 1/3 cup of low fat cream cheese
- ½ cup of low sodium chicken broth
- ½ cup of sharp cheddar cheese, shredded
- ¼ cup of green onions, thinly sliced
- ¼ cup of plum tomato, seeds removed and chopped
- ½ teaspoons of black pepper

HHHHHHHHHHHHHHHHHHHHHHHHHHHHHHHHH

Instructions:

1. Preheat the oven to 400 degrees.

2. Place the pierogies into a greased baking dish.

3. In a saucepan set over medium heat, add in the bacon. Cook for 5 minutes or until crispy. Remove and transfer onto a plate to drain. Once cooled, crumble the bacon.

4. In the saucepan, add in the garlic. Cook for 30 seconds.

5. Add in 1/3 cup of the low-fat cream cheese. Cook for an additional minute. Add in the chicken broth and stir well until smooth in consistency. Remove and pour over the pierogies.

6. Sprinkle ½ cup of the shredded cheddar cheese over the top.

7. Place into the oven to bake for 20 minutes. Remove from the oven.

8. Top off with the crumbled bacon, sliced green onions, chopped plum tomato and dash of black pepper.

Recipe 12: Ravioli and Roasted Zucchini

This is a delicious ravioli dish you can make whenever you are craving something on the healthy side.

Yield: 4 servings

Cooking Time: 40 minutes

Ingredient List:

- 4 zucchini, thinly sliced
- 2 Tablespoons of extra virgin olive oil
- 1 teaspoon of crushed red pepper flakes
- 2/3 cup of grated Parmesan cheese
- ¼ teaspoons of black pepper
- 2 Tablespoons of salt
- 2 cloves of garlic, crushed
- 1 pound of cheese ravioli
- 3 Tablespoons of flat leaf parsley, chopped

HHHHHHHHHHHHHHHHHHHHHHHHHHHHHHHH

Instructions:

1. Preheat the oven to 400 degrees.

2. In a pot set over medium to high heat, fill with salted water. Allow to come to a boil.

3. In a baking dish, add in the zucchini. Drizzle the olive oil, crushed red pepper flakes and 3 tablespoons of grated Parmesan cheese. Season with a dash of salt and black pepper. Stir well to mix.

4. Add the ravioli into the pot with the boiling water. Boil for 5 minutes or until soft. Drain and transfer into a bowl.

5. In the baking dish, add in the garlic. Place into the oven to bake for 20 minutes or until the zucchini is soft.

6. Remove from the oven. Add in the ravioli and toss gently to mix.

7. Serve with a topping of the chopped parsley and grated Parmesan cheese.

Recipe 13: Baked Broccoli Ravioli

This is the perfect ravioli dish for you to make whenever you are craving something on the healthier side.

Yield: 4 servings

Cooking Time: 1 hour

Ingredient List:

- 1 cup of basil leaves
- ½ cup of extra virgin olive oil
- 2 Tablespoons of extra virgin olive oil
- Extra virgin olive oil, as needed
- Dash of salt
- 2 cloves of garlic, minced
- 1 ½ pound of broccoli
- 1 tablespoon of butter, soft
- ½ cup of ricotta cheese
- ¼ cup of pecorino cheese, grated
- 3 Tablespoons of pecorino cheese, grated
- Pecorino cheese, grated
- ½ pound of lasagna sheets

HHHHHHHHHHHHHHHHHHHHHHHHHHHHHHHH

Instructions:

1. Add the basil leaves in a pot filled with boiling water. Boil for 20 seconds. Drain and rinse under water. Squeeze the leaves dry. Transfer into a mini food processor. Add in ½ cup of olive oil. Blend on the highest setting until pureed. Season with a dash of salt. Transfer into a bowl.

2. In a skillet set over medium to high heat, add in 2 tablespoons of extra virgin olive oil. Add in the minced garlic. Cook for 30 seconds.

3. Add in the broccoli, ½ cup of water and butter. Cover and cook for 10 minutes or until soft. Remove from heat and cool. Transfer into a food processor. Pulse on the highest setting until pureed. Transfer into a bowl. Add in the ricotta cheese and ¼ cup of the grated pecorino cheese. Season with a dash of salt. Stir well to mix.

4. In a pot set over medium to high heat, fill with water. Season with a dash of salt. Cut the lasagna sheets into 4 inch squares. Add into the pot and cook for 2 minutes or until soft. Dry and pat dry with a few paper towels.

5. Preheat the oven to 425 degrees. Grease a baking dish with 1 tablespoon of extra virgin olive oil.

6. Add two tablespoons of the filling in the center if each lasagna square. Fold the lasagna over the filling into triangles. Repeat. Place into the baking dish.

7. Sprinkle 3 tablespoons of pecorino cheese over the ravioli.

8. Place into the oven to bake for 10 minutes or until the cheese begins to turn brown.

9. Drizzle the basil and oil mix over the top.

10. Serve.

Recipe 14: Pesto, Squash and Sage Ravioli

This is a ravioli dish that is known for its simplicity yet amazing taste. While it is easy to make, it can be dressed up in any rich sauce you want to make.

Yield: 4 servings

Cooking Time: 18 minutes

Ingredient List:

- 8 ounces of butternut squash, chopped
- 12 ounces of cheese ravioli
- ¼ cup of pesto sauce
- 2 Tablespoons of extra virgin olive oil
- 16 sage leaves
- ¼ cup of walnuts, chopped
- ¼ cup of grated Parmesan cheese

HHHHHHHHHHHHHHHHHHHHHHHHHHHHHHHH

Instructions:

1. In a saucepan set over medium to high heat, fill with salted water. Allow to come to a boil. Add in the squash. Cook for 4 to 5 minutes. Drain and set aside.

2. Fill the saucepan again with salted water. Allow to come to a boil. Add in the cheese ravioli. Cook for 3 to 5 minutes or until the ravioli begins to float to the surface. Drain the ravioli and set aside.

3. In a skillet set over medium to high heat, add in 1 tablespoon of extra virgin olive oil. Add in the chopped squash, dash of salt and black pepper. Cook for 5 minutes. Transfer into a bowl.

4. In the same skillet, add another tablespoon of olive oil. Add in the sage leaves. Cook for 30 seconds or until crispy. Transfer onto a plate lined with paper towels to drain.

5. Spoon the squash over the cooked ravioli.

6. Serve with a garnish of grated parmesan cheese, chopped walnuts and cooked sage.

Recipe 15: Crabmeat Ravioli in Clam Sauce

This is the perfect ravioli dish to make for all of the seafood lovers out there. Feel free to make the sauce two days ahead of time to save yourself some time.

Yield: 6 servings

Cooking Time: 1 hour

Ingredients for the sauce:

- 1 tablespoon of extra virgin olive oil
- 1/3 cup of onion, chopped
- 2 cloves of garlic, minced
- 1, 28 ounce can of tomatoes, crushed
- 1, 14.5 ounce can of no salt tomatoes, chopped
- 2 Tablespoons of flat leaf parsley, chopped
- 1 tablespoon of oregano, chopped
- ¼ teaspoons of salt
- ¼ teaspoons of black pepper
- 1, 10 ounce can of clams, drained

Ingredients for the ravioli:

- ½ pound of lumpy crabmeat, shell pieces removed
- ½ cup of red bell pepper, chopped
- 2 Tablespoons of panko breadcrumbs
- 1 tablespoon of chives, chopped
- 1/8 teaspoons of salt
- ½ cup of ricotta cheese
- 24 wonton wrappers

HHHHHHHHHHHHHHHHHHHHHHHHHHHHHHHH

Instructions:

1. Prepare the sauce. In a Dutch oven set over medium to high heat, add in the olive oil. Add in the chopped onion. Cook for 5 minutes or until soft. Add in the minced garlic and cook for an additional minute.

2. Add in the cans of crushed and chopped tomatoes. Allow to come to a boil. Lower the heat to low. Cook for 30 minutes.

3. Add in the chopped parsley, chopped oregano, dash of salt, black pepper and can of drained clams. Stir to mix. Cook for 10 minutes.

4. Remove from heat and set aside.

5. Prepare the ravioli. In a bowl, add in the crab meat, chopped red bell pepper, panko breadcrumbs, chopped chives and dash of salt. Stir well to mix. Add in the ricotta cheese and stir well to incorporate.

6. On the wonton wrappers, add 1 tablespoon of the crab filling. Fold the wrappers over the filling and crimp the edges to seal. Repeat.

7. In a Dutch oven set over medium to high heat, fill with salted water. Allow to come to a boil. Add in the ravioli. Cook for 5 minutes or until cooked through. Drain and transfer into the sauce. Stir gently to mix.

8. Serve immediately.

Recipe 16: Three Bean Ravioli Minestrone

Make this delicious minestrone whenever you are feeling a bit under the weather. It is made with plenty of vegetables and beans to make a hearty and healthy dish you won't have to feel guilty about enjoying.

Yield: 10 servings

Cooking Time: 40 minutes

Ingredient List:

- 1 tablespoon of extra virgin olive oil
- 1 onion, chopped
- 2 carrots, chopped
- 2 ribs of celery, thinly sliced
- 2 cloves of garlic, minced
- 3, 14 ounce cans of chicken broth
- 1, 9 ounce pack of baby lime beans
- 1, 16 ounce of light red kidney beans, drained
- 1, 16 ounce can of garbanzo beans, drained
- 2, 14.5 ounce cans of tomatoes, chopped
- 2 teaspoons of Italian seasoning
- 1 teaspoon of black pepper
- ½ teaspoons of salt
- 1, 7 ounce pack of miniature cheese ravioli
- Parmesan cheese, shredded

HHHHHHHHHHHHHHHHHHHHHHHHHHHHHHHH

Instructions:

1. In a stockpot set over medium heat, add in all of the ingredients except for the shredded parmesan cheese and cheese ravioli. Stir gently to mix.

2. Cover and cook for 30 minutes.

3. Add in the miniature cheese ravioli. Continue to cook for 10 minutes or until soft.

4. Remove from heat.

5. Serve with a topping of the shredded parmesan cheese.

Recipe 17: Ravioli with Brown Butter and Roasted Squash

This is a simple and delicious ravioli dish you can make whenever you are craving something that won't take you much time to put together.

Yield: 6 servings

Cooking Time: 55 minutes

Ingredient List:

- 1 ½ pound of butternut squash, chopped
- 1 tablespoon of extra virgin olive oil
- 30 jumbo 4 cheese ravioli
- 1 stick of butter, soft
- ½ of an onion, chopped
- 24 sage leaves, whole
- ½ cup of grated Parmesan cheese
- ¼ teaspoons of salt
- ¼ teaspoons of black pepper

HHHHHHHHHHHHHHHHHHHHHHHHHHHHHHH

Instructions:

1. Preheat the oven to 475 degrees.

2. On a baking sheet, add the chopped butternut squash and olive oil. Toss well until coated. Place into the oven to bake for 25 minutes or until soft. Remove and set aside.

3. In a pot set over medium to high heat, fill with salted water. Allow to come to a boil. Add in the ravioli. Cook for 5 minutes or until soft. Drain the ravioli and set aside.

4. In a skillet set over medium heat, add in the butter. Add in the chopped onion. Cook for 5 minutes or until soft. Add in the sage leaves and continue to cook for 3 minutes or until the butter begins to smell nutty.

5. Transfer the ravioli onto serving plates. Top off with the roasted squash and grated Parmesan cheese.

6. Pour the brown butter and sage mix over the top. Season with a dash of salt and black pepper.

7. Serve.

Recipe 18: Goat Cheese Stuffed Mint Ravioli

This is a ravioli dish that is worth making completely from scratch. It is packed with small bursts of flavor, I know you will want to make it as often as possible.

Yield: 6 servings

Cooking Time: 1 hour and 25 minutes

Ingredients for the pasta:

- 2 cups of mint, chopped
- 3 eggs, beaten
- 2 cups of all-purpose flour
- ½ teaspoons of salt
- 1 teaspoon of extra virgin olive oil
- 3 Tablespoons of warm water

Ingredients for the filling:

- 2 cups of ricotta cheese
- 1 cup of goat cheese, crumbled
- ¼ teaspoons of salt
- Dash of black pepper

Ingredients for serving:

- 2 ounces of butter
- Lemon zest, grated
- Mint sprigs, for garnish

HHHHHHHHHHHHHHHHHHHHHHHHHHHHHHH

Instructions:

1. Prepare the pasta. In a saucepan set over medium heat, fill with water. Add in the mint. Cook for 1 minute or until bright green. Drain the mint leaves and set aside to cool completely.

2. In a food processor, add in the beaten eggs and mint. Pulse on the highest setting until chopped.

3. On a flat surface, add the all-purpose flour and dash of salt. Add in the egg mix, extra virgin olive oil and water. Stir well until a dough begins to form. Knead the dough for 10 to 15 minutes or until smooth in consistency.

4. Wrap the dough in plastic wrap. Set aside to rest for 1 hour.

5. Prepare the filling. In a bowl, add in the ricotta cheese, crumbled goat cheese, dash of salt and black pepper. Beat with an electric mixer until smooth in consistency.

6. Divide the dough into 4 pieces. Feed each piece of dough into a pasta machine on the widest setting. Then pass the dough twice on the #6 setting. Cover the dough and set aside to rest.

7. Use a biscuit cutter, cut out 3 ½ inch sized circles from the dough.

8. Spoon 1 tablespoon of the filling into the center of each dough round. Cover the filling with another pasta round and crimp the edges to seal. Repeat with the remaining dough and filling.

9. In a saucepan set over medium heat, fill with salted water. Allow to come to a boil. Add in the ravioli and cook for 1 to 2 minutes or until the ravioli begins to float to the surface. Drain and set aside.

10. In a skillet set over medium heat, add 2 tablespoons of butter. Add in the ravioli. Cook for 2 minutes or until golden. Transfer onto a plate.

11. Serve with a garnish of lemon zest and the mint sprigs.

Recipe 19: Garlic and Herb Oil Ravioli

This is a restaurant quality meal that only takes a few minutes to prepare. Made with ravioli, pepper flakes, parsley and garlic, it is a simple yet delicious dish I know you will love.

Yield: 4 servings

Cooking Time: 20 minutes

Ingredient List:

- 1 pack of cheese ravioli
- ¼ cup of extra virgin olive oil
- 1 clove of garlic, minced
- ¼ teaspoons of crushed red pepper flakes
- ¼ cup of flat leaf parsley, chopped
- 2 Tablespoons of chives, chopped
- Dash of salt

HHHHHHHHHHHHHHHHHHHHHHHHHHHHHHHH

Instructions:

1. Prepare the cheese ravioli according to the directions on the package. Drain the ravioli and place back into the pot.

2. In a saucepan set over medium heat, add in the extra virgin olive oil, minced garlic and crushed red pepper flakes. Cook for 1 minute or until the garlic is gold. Remove from heat.

3. Add the cheese ravioli to the saucepan. Toss gently to mix.

4. Add in the chopped chives, chopped parsley and a dash of salt. Toss gently to mix.

5. Serve immediately.

Recipe 20: Tuscan Ravioli with Tomato and Basil Sauce

This is a delicious ravioli dish you can serve to make an elegant Italian dinner for your significant other.

Yield: 4 to 6 servings

Cooking Time: 15 minutes

Ingredient List:

- 1, 20 ounce pack of four cheese ravioli
- 1, 16 ounce jar of sundried tomato alfredo sauce
- 2 Tablespoons of dried white wine
- 2 tomatoes, chopped
- ½ cup of basil, chopped
- 1/3 cup of grated parmesan cheese
- Basil strips, for garnish

HHHHHHHHHHHHHHHHHHHHHHHHHHHHHHHHH

Instructions:

1. Prepare the four cheese ravioli according to the directions on the package.

2. In a saucepan set over medium heat, add in the tomato and alfredo sauce. Add in the dried white wine, chopped tomatoes and chopped basil. Stir well to mix. Cook for 5 minutes or until hot.

3. Add in the prepared ravioli and toss gently to coat.

4. Sprinkle the grated parmesan cheese over the top.

5. Remove from heat. Serve with a garnish of basil strips.

Recipe 21: Ravioli and Vegetable Soup

Make this delicious ravioli dish whenever you are craving something warm to enjoy on a cold winter night.

Yield: 4 servings

Cooking Time: 25 minutes

Ingredient List:

- 1 tablespoon of extra virgin olive oil
- 2 cups of bell pepper and onion mix, chopped
- 2 cloves of garlic, minced
- ¼ teaspoons of crushed red pepper flakes
- 1, 28 ounce can of fire-roasted crushed tomatoes
- 1, 15 ounce can of vegetable broth
- 1 ½ cups of hot water
- 1 teaspoon of dried basil
- 1, 6 to 9 ounce pack of cheese ravioli
- 2 cups of zucchini, chopped
- Dash of black pepper

HHHHHHHHHHHHHHHHHHHHHHHHHHHHHHHH

Instructions:

1. In a Dutch oven set over medium heat, add in the olive oil. Add in the chopped onion mix, minced garlic and crushed red pepper flakes. Stir well to mix. Cook for 1 minute.

2. Add in the can of crushed tomatoes, vegetable broth, water and dried basil. Stir well to mix. Allow to come to a boil.

3. Add in the cheese ravioli. Cook for 3 minutes or until the ravioli begins to float to the surface.

4. Add in the chopped zucchini. Allow to come back to a boil. Cook for 3 minutes or until the zucchini is soft.

5. Season with a dash of salt and black pepper.

6. Remove from heat and serve immediately.

Recipe 22: Cheese Ravioli with Cherry Tomato Sauce

This is a simple yet delicious ravioli dish you can make whenever you want to spoil your significant other. For the best results, use fresh cherry tomatoes.

Yield: 4 servings

Cooking Time: 55 minutes

Ingredient List:

- 1 cup of ricotta cheese
- ¾ ounces of grated Parmigiano-Reggiano cheese
- 1 teaspoon of thyme, minced
- 1/3 cup of flat-leaf parsley, chopped
- ½ teaspoons of lemon zest, minced
- Dash of salt and black pepper
- 1 egg, separated
- ¼ cup of extra virgin olive oil
- 1 tablespoon of garlic, minced
- 1 pint of cherry tomatoes, stems removed and cut into halves
- 2 Tablespoons of basil, thinly sliced

Ingredients for the pasta:

- 2 ¼ cups of all-purpose flour
- 3 eggs, beaten
- Semolina flour, for dusting

HHHHHHHHHHHHHHHHHHHHHHHHHHHHHHHH

Instructions:

1. In a bowl, add in the ricotta cheese, grated Parmigiano-Reggiano cheese, minced thyme, chopped parsley, minced lemon zest and egg yolk. Season with a dash of salt and black pepper. Stir well to mix.

2. In a separate bowl, add in the egg white.

3. Prepare the pasta. Add 2 ¼ cups of all-purpose flour onto a flat surface. Add the beaten eggs and fold the flour to even mix. Knead the dough for 5 minutes or until smooth in consistency. Divide the dough in half. Pass the dough through pasta rollers until 1/16 inch in thickness.

4. Use a 3 inch biscuit cutter and cut out rounds from the dough.

5. In each round of dough, add 1 teaspoon of the cheese filling in the center. Add another pasta round over the filling and seal the edges. Repeat with the remaining dough and filling.

6. In a saucepan set over medium heat, add the olive oil. Add in the minced garlic. Cook for 2 minutes. Add in the chopped cherry tomatoes. Cook for 3 to 5 minutes or until the tomatoes begin to brown. Season with a dash of salt and black pepper.

7. In a pot set over high heat, fill with salted water. Allow to come to a boil. Add in the ravioli. Cook for 12 minutes or until soft. Drain the ravioli and transfer into the sauce. Add in the sliced basil and toss gently to coat.

8. Remove from heat and serve immediately.

Recipe 23: Cherry and Brown Butter Ravioli

The cherries used in this dish help to give it a delicious sweetness that is impossible to resist. It is great for those who need to satisfy a strong sweet tooth.

Yield: 4 servings

Cooking Time: 45 minutes

Ingredient List:

- 10 ounces of cheese ravioli
- ½ cup of butter
- 3 Tablespoons of lemon juice
- ½ teaspoons of salt
- 3 cups of Rainier cherries, pits removed and sliced into halves
- ¼ cup of almonds, toasted and chopped
- 1 tablespoon of thyme leaves

HHHHHHHHHHHHHHHHHHHHHHHHHHHHHHHH

Instructions:

1. Prepare the cheese ravioli according to the directions on the package. Drain the ravioli and set aside onto a plate.

2. In a saucepan set over high heat, add in the butter. Once it melts, lower the heat to low and cook for 8 minutes or until the butter turns brown. Remove from heat. Add in the lemon juice, and dash of salt. Stir well to mix. Pour into a bowl and set aside.

3. Add the cherries into the saucepan. Cook for 8 minutes or until the skin begins to wrinkle.

4. Pour the brown butter and cherries over the cooked ravioli.

5. Sprinkle the chopped almonds and thyme leaves over the top.

6. Serve.

Recipe 24: Pumpkin Ravioli with Gorgonzola Sauce

This is a new way to use pumpkin during the fall season. Make sure to serve this delicious ravioli dish with a glass of chardonnay.

Yield: 6 servings

Cooking Time: 15 minutes

Ingredient List:

- 1 ¼ cups of canned pumpkin
- 2 Tablespoons of dried breadcrumbs
- 2 Tablespoons of grated Parmesan cheese
- ½ teaspoons of salt
- ½ teaspoons of sage, minced
- ¼ teaspoons of black pepper
- 1/8 teaspoons of powdered nutmeg
- 30 round wonton wrappers
- 1 tablespoon of cornstarch
- 1 cup of fat free milk
- 1 tablespoon of all-purpose flour
- 1 ½ Tablespoons of butter
- ½ cup of Gorgonzola cheese, crumbled
- 3 Tablespoons of hazelnuts, chopped and toasted

HHHHHHHHHHHHHHHHHHHHHHHHHHHHHHHH

Instructions:

1. Scoop the pumpkin onto a flat surface. Spread until ½ inch in thickness. Cover with paper towels and set aside to rest for 5 minutes. Scrape into a bowl.

2. In the bowl, add in the dried breadcrumbs, grated Parmesan cheese, dash of salt, minced sage, black pepper and powdered nutmeg. Stir well to mix.

3. On the wonton wrappers, add 2 teaspoons of the pumpkin mix into the center. Fold the skin over the filling and crimp the edges to seal. Repeat. Transfer onto a baking sheet dusted with cornstarch.

4. In a Dutch oven set over medium to high heat, fill with water and allow to come to a simmer. Add in the ravioli. Cook for 5 minutes or until soft. Drain and set aside.

5. In a saucepan set over medium heat, add in the fat free milk and all-purpose flour. Whisk until smooth in consistency. Allow to come to a boil. Cook for 1 minute or until thick in consistency. Remove from heat. Add in the butter and crumbled Gorgonzola cheese. Stir well to incorporate.

6. Place the ravioli onto serving plate. Pour the gorgonzola mix over the top.

7. Sprinkle the hazelnuts over the top and serve.

Recipe 25: Spinach Ravioli Lasagna

This is a delicious lasagna recipe for you to make whenever you need to feed a large group of people. It is a delicious main dish that you can make that requires little effort to put together.

Yield: 6 to 8 servings

Cooking Time: 45 minutes

Ingredient List:

- 1, 6 ounce pack of baby spinach, washed
- 1/3 cup of pesto sauce
- 1, 15 ounce jar of alfredo sauce
- ¼ cup of vegetable broth
- 1, 25 ounce pack of cheese ravioli
- 1 cup of Italian size cheese blend, shredded
- Basil, chopped and for garnish
- Smoked paprika, for garnish

HHHHHHHHHHHHHHHHHHHHHHHHHHHHHHH

Instructions:

1. Preheat the oven to 375 degrees.

2. In a bowl, add in the pesto sauce and chopped spinach. Toss well until coated.

3. In a bowl, add the alfredo sauce and vegetable broth. Stir well to mix. Pour 1/3 of the sauce into a greased baking dish.

4. Top off with half of the spinach mix. Add half of the cheese ravioli over the spinach. Repeat these layers once more. Top off with the remaining alfredo sauce mix.

5. Place into the oven to bake for 30 minutes.

6. Remove and sprinkle the remaining shredded Italian cheese over the top. Place back into the oven to bake for 5 minutes.

7. Remove from the oven. Serve with a garnish of chopped basil and smoked paprika.

About the Author

Angel Burns learned to cook when she worked in the local seafood restaurant near her home in Hyannis Port in Massachusetts as a teenager. The head chef took Angel under his wing and taught the young woman the tricks of the trade for cooking seafood. The skills she had learned at a young age helped her get accepted into Boston University's Culinary Program where she also minored in business administration.

Summers off from school meant working at the same restaurant but when Angel's mentor and friend retired as head chef, she took over after graduation and created classic and new dishes that delighted the diners. The restaurant flourished under Angel's culinary creativity and one customer developed more than an appreciation for Angel's food. Several months after taking over the position, the young woman met her future husband at work and they have been inseparable ever since. They still live in Hyannis Port with their two children and a cocker spaniel named Buddy.

Angel Burns turned her passion for cooking and her business acumen into a thriving e-book business. She has authored several successful books on cooking different types of dishes using simple ingredients for novices and experienced chefs alike. She is still head chef in Hyannis Port and says she will probably never leave!

Author's Afterthoughts

With so many books out there to choose from, I want to thank you for choosing this one and taking precious time out of your life to buy and read my work. Readers like you are the reason I take such passion in creating these books.

It is with gratitude and humility that I express how honored I am to become a part of your life and I hope that you take the same pleasure in reading this book as I did in writing it.

Can I ask one small favour? I ask that you write an honest and open review on Amazon of what you thought of the book. This will help other readers make an informed choice on whether to buy this book.

My sincerest thanks,

Angel Burns

If you want to be the first to know about news, new books, events and giveaways, subscribe to my newsletter by clicking the link below

https://angel-burns.gr8.com

or Scan QR-code

Printed in Great Britain
by Amazon